essential careers™

A Career as an

OPERATING AND STATIONARY ENGINEER

Kerry Hinton

ROSEN PUBLISHING

NEW YORK

Published in 2016 by The Rosen Publishing Group, Inc.
29 East 21st Street, New York, NY 10010

Library of Congress CataloginginPublication Data

Hinton, Kerry, author.
 A career as an operating and stationary engineer / Kerry Hinton. -- First edition.
     pages cm. -- (Essential careers)
 Includes bibliographical references and index.
 ISBN 978-1-4994-6223-4 (library bound)
1. Mechanical engineering--Vocational guidance--Juvenile literature. 2. Steam
engineering--Vocational guidance--Juvenile literature. 3. Electrical engineering--
Vocational guidance--Juvenile literature. 4. Maintenance--Juvenile literature. 5.
Building trades--Juvenile literature. 6. Mechanical engineers--Juvenile literature. I.
Title. II. Series: Essential careers.
 TJ157.H56 2016
 620.0023--dc23
                                2015021799

Manufactured in the United States of America

contents

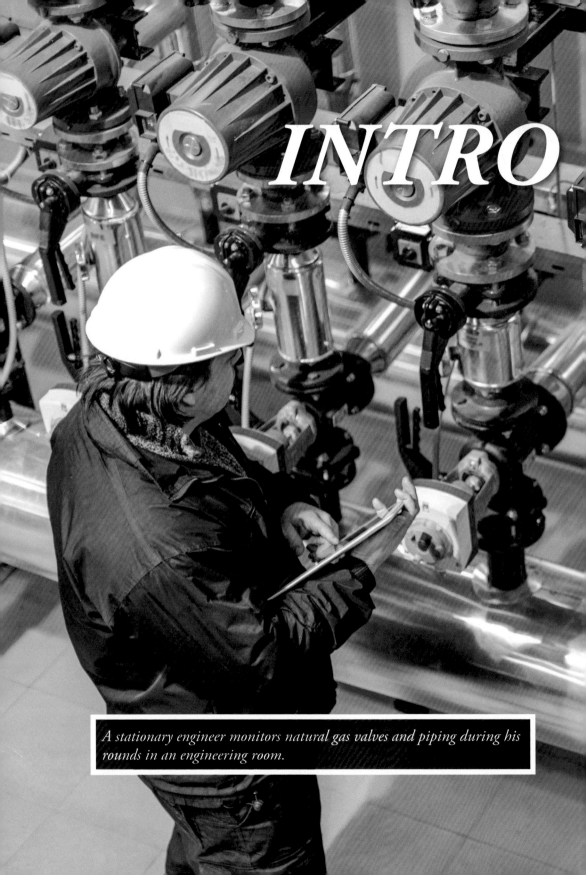

INTRO

A stationary engineer monitors natural gas valves and piping during his rounds in an engineering room.

DUCTION

Operating and stationary engineers help keep the world running smoothly every day. We may not always notice them, but they are working around the clock doing work most of us rarely consider. Some are on work sites behind orange safety fences, driving bulldozers and backhoes. Some are completely out of sight, working in equipment and auxiliary rooms filled with lights and vibrating equipment. These men and women do not only operate these mighty machines, but also ensure they operate safely.

What type of machines? These are the machines of great industry. They move earth and rock. They start and control great fires. They run the equipment that runs the world. These are the machines that have helped the United States, Canada, and the rest of the world to progress to where they are today.

Some of these machines may be found on construction sites. They perform many tasks—anything from lifting steel beams to repairing bridges and tunnels to smoothing out earth.

Many machines are essential to daily life; they enable people to work, travel, and communicate. Large power plants for example, provide electricity to power our lights and televisions. Air-conditioning systems keep apartment buildings comfortable and computer servers cool. If these machines stopped working, people wouldn't be able to enjoy many of the benefits of modern life they take for granted every day.

People use electricity at all hours of the day; someone is always turning on a light somewhere! Hospitals need lights for surgery and examining patients, for example. Stationary engineers and their supervisors make sure that power plants stay online to deliver power to a city and its suburbs. Suppose that same hospital also needs steam for sterilizing surgical instruments. This would require a stationary engineer in the building to maintain the steam system and make repairs if needed.

A career as an operating or stationary engineer is both mentally and physically challenging. Knowledge of math and science is necessary, as is close attention to detail. Many situations in this line of work involve problem solving, so a curiosity about the way things work is also helpful.

Physically, operating and stationary engineers spend much of their days in motion and in noisy environments. Heavy lifting and high heat levels are common. Construction vehicles vibrate and shake and make so much noise that operators usually need hearing protection. Engineering spaces where steam and electricity are made are hot and loud as well. This profession is not for people who desire a peaceful and quiet workday.

Working in this environment is a huge responsibility. Heavy equipment can fail and break, steam boilers can explode, and other large machines can hurt people very easily if they are used incorrectly. This is why learning to become an operating or stationary engineer takes at least four years of training combined with more training—actual experience with the equipment. Learning never stops in this profession. As technology changes, so do the jobs of operating and stationary engineers. This means that retraining to adapt or learn new equipment or methods of doing things is not only smart but necessary.

Construction and power are both incredibly important to the world today. Yes, the technology of buildings and power may change, but there will always be a need for people with basic engineering skills. People will always live and work in buildings; those buildings need light and heat. Operating and stationary engineers are always working to keep our walls up and our power on.

Do you like to be part of a team that works toward a bigger goal? Do you like to solve puzzles? Do you like physical and mental challenges? If any of these sound interesting, then a career in stationary engineering is definitely worth exploring.

chapter 1

What Are Operating and Stationary Engineers?

Before you decide if you'd like to pursue a career as an operating or stationary engineer, it may be useful to look more closely at what each career involves. If you opened a dictionary and looked up the word "engineer," you would find a few different definitions. Not all engineers are the same, so it is important to know what sort of engineers this book will discuss.

It may be helpful to discuss what operating and stationary engineers are *not*:

- **Professional engineers.** A professional engineer uses math and science to create and build things to improve everyday life. He or she must complete a four-year college engineering program and training before becoming licensed. This process takes about eight years. After licensing, professional engineers are able to design machines, plan buildings, or develop systems in those buildings. A professional engineer's final approval on a design means he or she is responsible for its overall safety.
- **Railroad engineers.** These men and women operate and assist trains that run on rails and carry passengers or cargo.

- **Marine engineers.** Marine engineers work in places such as on boats, ships, and oil rigs. Some people in this line of work may also have professional engineering training.

Operating and stationary engineers are different from the engineers listed above. They use and care for the systems, buildings, and machines that professional engineers design. For this reason, it is common to find people from different fields working together on certain projects. For instance, an operational engineer may be employed in the construction of a building designed by a professional engineer. Each job relies on the other for a project to be completed properly and on time.

A career in operating and stationary engineering is called a trade. A trade is a job that requires specific skills that are obtained by hours and hours of supervised training. Professions like plumbing, carpentry, and welding are also considered trades. The jobs of operating and stationary engineers are so closely linked that they both share a trade union called the International Union of Operating Engineers (IUOE).

Both operating and stationary engineers work in industrial environments. This means that there is plenty of noise, heat, steam, and flammable material in their work areas. Large equipment and fuel can be dangerous, and appropriate protection is needed at all times.

We know that operating and stationary engineers are different from other kinds of engineers, but how can we tell them apart from one another? In the simplest terms, operating engineers use machines to bring buildings and construction projects to life. Stationary engineers help keep those buildings and machines running safely and efficiently. Of course, there are many more differences between operating and stationary engineers that can't be put into one sentence. Let's examine them.

An employee of New York City's Metropolitan Transit Authority (MTA) transports workers in a locomotive underneath the surface of Manhattan.

OPERATING ENGINEERS

Operating engineers usually work outside. This may be enjoyable in sunny weather, but expect to be exposed to all the elements if you choose this profession.

Unlike U.S. Postal Service letter carriers, operating engineers can be greatly affected by weather. Sometimes weather conditions may be tolerable but still too extreme to use heavy equipment. In some cases, it may too dangerous to be on a worksite at all. If bad weather occurs it could mean that an operating engineer may spend some time employed but not working. Not all weather will stop construction, but heavy rain, snow, hurricanes, lightning, and tornadoes are all examples of extreme weather that could shut down a project. Conditions like these have a serious effect on people, machines, and the earth itself and make it difficult to work safely.

Operating engineers usually belong to one of three

A heavy equipment operator maneuvers a bulldozer on a construction site. These operating engineers must be able to operate the many machines used on construction sites.

specialties. All are equally important to completing a project and need each other to fully do their jobs.

The first type of operating engineer is known as a construction equipment operator. These engineers do exactly what their job title describes. They operate all of the vehicles and machines on a construction work site. These include cranes, backhoes, pavers, and bulldozers, but there are dozens of types of machines and vehicles used in construction.

Heavy vehicle service technicians support the team by making sure heavy equipment operators have working equipment to use. If equipment shuts down, an entire job could shut down.

Technical surveyors are also sometimes called map technicians. They spend their days figuring out and marking the actual physical boundaries of blueprints and project plans. They also determine where buildings and structures will be placed. If it weren't for surveyors, heavy equipment operators wouldn't know where, when, or how to do their work on a site.

ENERGY

Energy powers everything on our planet. Yes, everything, including people and animals. When we eat food, it gives us energy to ride a bike, jog, and throw a Frisbees. When we eat, our bodies convert food to energy. If we forget to eat, our bodies don't work correctly. Why? Not enough energy.

Machines also need energy to work. Their food is fuel. There are many types of fuel to use in machines. Not all devices and tools use the same type. In this resource, we will mainly be discussing the three most common fuels in the field of operating and stationary engineering: coal, oil, and natural gas. All three come from the earth. When they are burned they provide heat energy that is then used to move engine parts and vehicles.

Two survey technicians on a construction site take measurements to ensure the project will be built on a level surface.

Since engineering licenses differ depending on the state or province, some of these jobs and qualifications may have different names, but the work and training are essentially the same.

STATIONARY ENGINEERS

The word "stationary" means not moving, but this does not mean stationary engineers stand still at work. The term refers to the equipment that is used on the job. Since none of it is used to move a vehicle or boat, it is all considered stationary equipment.

Do moving engineers exist? Yes, but they are called marine engineers and they work on tugboats, ocean liners, and navy ships. Their jobs involve keeping boats and ships afloat and powered. Marine engineers sometimes have similar training as stationary engineers, but their careers are not similar enough for them to train or work together.

The technology used by stationary engineers (known as power engineers in Canada) was born on the lakes, rivers, and oceans of North America. The first powerful steam engines were used to power boats in the early 1800s. Steam engines are used to this day in the navy, Coast Guard, and Merchant Marine. Today, it is common for marine engineers to leave or retire from the navy or Merchant Marine

An HVACR technician performs maintenance on a piece of refrigeration equipment. HVACR technicians are one type of stationary engineer.

and train to be stationary engineers. From the steamboat to today's navy warships, steam engines are as important as ever.

According to Russell Duke of the International Union of Operating Engineers, stationary engineers are responsible for  "the entire indoor environment." This means light, heat, power, and climate control. This is such a broad job that specialties are necessary for every piece of equipment to work properly. Duke adds that stationary engineers are usually "behind the scenes until something breaks. If you are in a building that's run well, you seldom or never see them."

Now that we can define both operating and stationary engineering, let's take a look at the jobs they do today as well as where their specialties are heading in the future.

SAFETY FIRST

Workplace safety is very important for operating and stationary engineers. That is why the Occupational Health & Safety Administration (OSHA) was formed in 1970. OSHA is part of the Department of Labor, and its mission is to help employers and employees reduce on-the-job injuries, illnesses, and deaths.

There are so many hazards to be aware of and to avoid. According to a 2013 study by the U.S. Bureau of Labor Statistics, twelve people die every day in workplaces around the United States. This may not seem like a large number, but over the course of one year that number grows to more than 4,300 deaths. There are fewer people in Canada, but the country certainly felt the loss of 977 people in 2012, according to a 2013 Association of Workers' Compensation Boards of Canada (AWCBC) study.

OSHA also tells us that the greatest dangers to heavy equipment operators and mechanics are falls. In 2013, one in three construction deaths in the United States was caused by a fatal fall. Almost everything in a workspace or job site can be dangerous, however. Boilers can leak and spray hot liquid or steam. Fires can start in furnaces and steamroller engines. Aside from fire and other emergencies, the daily business of operating machines is also hazardous to engineer health. Most pieces of heavy equipment have dozens of moving parts that can catch skin or clothing. Diesel and petroleum fumes can cause nausea and serious health problems.

Electrical safety is very important as well. In addition to driving vehicles, operating engineers use electrical tools that can be dangerous. Workers on job sites and machine spaces also need to be aware of other dangers. Electrocution and flying objects are just a couple of the threats operational and stationary engineers face.

Employers must follow OSHA workplace regulations or be subject to fines. A willful violation (disobeying a rule on purpose) can result in a fine of up of to $70,000. OSHA provides all workers with guidelines for appropriate personal protective equipment (PPE) in the workplace. Street clothes and dangling jewelry are not allowed! PPE used by both operating an stationary engineers can include:

- Hardhats
- Fire-resistant protective clothing (normally overalls)
- Safety shoes with steel toes
- Safety glasses
- Breathing protection
- Hearing protection
- Chemical-resistant gloves

Engineering spaces are also well equipped with firefighting equipment. Many liquids in these spaces can create fires that cannot be extinguished with water. These guidelines apply to maintenance and repair work also. A machine that has been turned off can remain hot for hours, not to mention the hot liquids that flow through engines and boilers. It may also take time for an electric charge to leave some equipment, even after it has been powered down.

chapter 2

THE PAST, PRESENT, AND FUTURE

In order to understand where operating and stationary engineering careers are now, it is necessary to learn a little about the history of the machines that they rely on. Some of the basic principles from a few hundred years ago are still being used in engineering spaces and projects today.

THE INDUSTRIAL REVOLUTION IN NORTH AMERICA

Until the mid-1700s, people in North America and Europe lived very simple lives. Many lived in rural areas and worked their own small farms. Children stayed home and worked for their families. People made many of their own goods, but in their own homes and in small amounts. Technology was very limited during these years.

In the late eighteenth century, incredible advances occurred in the way things were made. A series of technological innovations known as the Industrial Revolution occurred first in England and then spread to other parts of Europe and North America. In 1790, America's first cotton mill opened. The mill used water power to spin raw cotton into yarn, which was used to make clothing. Since a mill could spin cotton hundreds of times faster than a human being, more companies built mills and spun cotton to sell. This was the beginning of manufacturing in North America, and these were some of the first factories on the continent. This was the beginning of industry.

Great advances were made in the making of iron during this time, also. Iron was used to build bridges and ships, and maybe most important, steam engines. Coal was used to make iron, and steam engines were used to pull coal from underground mines. Every part of this system was necessary for each aspect to develop. As steam engines began to increase in size, so did the amount of iron that could be made.

Incredible progress was also made in construction from this time through the 1800s. New transportation systems came about. Tools and techniques that would change engineering were invented, including paved roads, dynamite, and the profession of surveying.

The new machines and ideas of the Industrial Revolution enabled people to make and do more, which helped the world to grow. As the world grew, new discoveries in science and technology helped it grow

Operating and stationary engineers trace their origins to the Industrial Revolution. Slater Mill, the first cotton mill in the United States, was built in 1793.

COAL

Coal is the oldest known fossil fuel. It has been in use since about 2000 BCE and is still a popular source of heat today. Coal fires many of the boilers that make electricity in America, Canada, and around the world.

If someone tells you that coal comes from the bones of dinosaurs, gently let them know that they are incorrect! Coal does come from the earth, but it is formed from dead plant matter such as plants, trees, bark, and other vegetation.

After millions of years of pressure and heat, this plant matter became the black rock-like fuel that runs steam engines and fills certain Christmas stockings. If you examine a piece of coal closely, you may be able to see the fossils of the leaves and stems that were alive when they first began their journey to become an energy source.

Coal is nonrenewable. This means that when the world's coal supply is gone, there will be no way to manufacture any more. According to a 2013 article by World Coal Organization, the world has a little over one hundred years of coal reserves left.

Of course, today there are other ways to start a fire. This means that if and when the coal reserves are empty there will be other fuels to use. But the price of coal is cheap and very stable, so it is still the most common fuel used in electrical generation. The United States and Canada produce two billion pounds of coal per year.

even more. An advance in one machine could solve a problem with another developing machine, which improved life greatly in a small amount of time. The Industrial Revolution lasted about eighty years, but there were more advances in those years than there had been in the previous three hundred.

THE BIRTH OF STATIONARY AND OPERATIONAL ENGINEERING

In 1763, a man named James Watt made some major improvements on an engine that had been invented almost seventy years before. He made his engine smaller and more powerful and used it to pump water from coal mines. In the years that followed, many people thought Watt's steam engine could be modified for other uses. Making the engine more powerful was the next step. Forty-one years later, the first steam engine was used to power a train in 1804. Using steam engines on the water was not far behind; three years later, Robert Fulton launched the *North River Steamboat.*

Steam engines were used only for transportation for about one hundred years more. Steam turbines and diesel engines replaced the steam engine at sea in the early twentieth century.

In power plants, steam engines stayed in operation. Pearl Street Station, the first central power plant that sent electricity to multiple homes, was built in 1882. It powered eighty-two customers in New York City. By 1930, more than seventy-seven million people had electricity in their homes.

Today, most power plants are steam-electric. The original steam engines from the early days of power generation have been replaced by steam turbines, which have fewer moving parts and are more efficient.

As with stationary engineering, steam played an important part in the development of operational engineering. Before heavy equipment was invented, people used their arms and handmade equipment to perform tasks that machines now do in a fraction of the time.

The first real piece of modern construction equipment was the Otis steam shovel, which was patented in 1839. It was used to move heavy dirt and rock that dozens of men could not. It

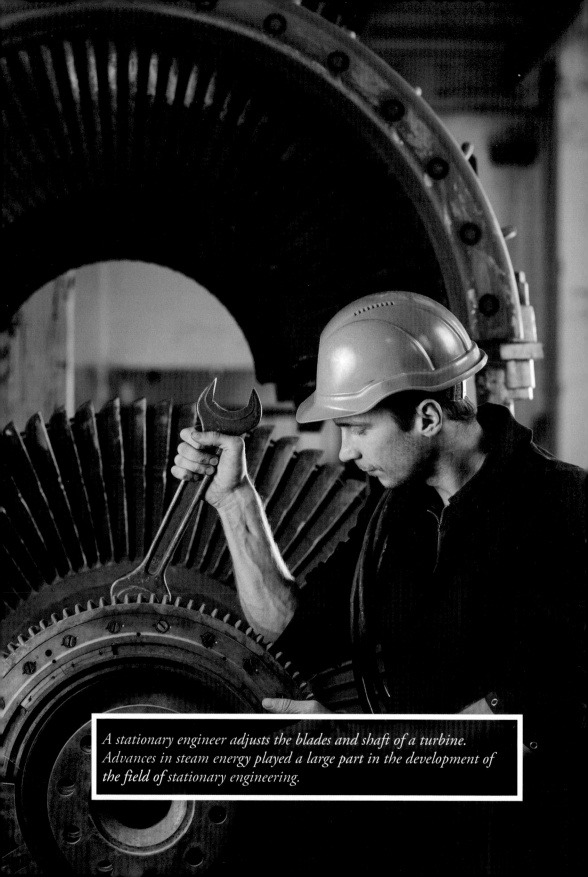

A stationary engineer adjusts the blades and shaft of a turbine. Advances in steam energy played a large part in the development of the field of stationary engineering.

was a multipurpose machine, used to dig canals and foundations of dams, as well as mine coal, iron, and copper. The steam shovel also played a key role in the construction of highways and railways in the United States and Canada.

THE INVENTIONS OF ROBERT FULTON

People sometimes call Robert Fulton the inventor of the steamboat, but this is not completely true. In the late 1700s, many inventors were working to improve upon the steam engine so it could power large boats. The launch of the *North River Steamboat* in 1807 was not the very first steamboat launch. The *North River Steamboat* was simply the first steamboat to succeed at operating as a business. The craft ran a regular route carrying passengers from New York City to Albany, New York. The steamboat's speed was less than 5 miles per hour (8 kilometers per hour)!

A few years before the launch of the *North River Steamboat*, Fulton did invent another watercraft: the submarine. With the help of the French government, the *Nautilus* sailed up Paris's Seine River in the summer of 1800.

Four years later, Robert Fulton moved to England to build weapons for the Royal Navy. This was surprising, since England was at war with Spain and France. One of the weapons Fulton designed for the British was the torpedo, which could be fired underwater to attack boats, other submarines, and targets on land. Torpedoes and the submarines that carry them are still used by the American and Canadian navies today.

By the time his "non-invention" launched in 1807, Robert Fulton had changed the future of naval warfare with two inventions he is *not* remembered for.

Over the next seventy-five to eighty years, dozens of machines and new construction techniques were invented. Each one brought operational engineering one step closer to the present. By the 1930s, the steam shovel was no longer

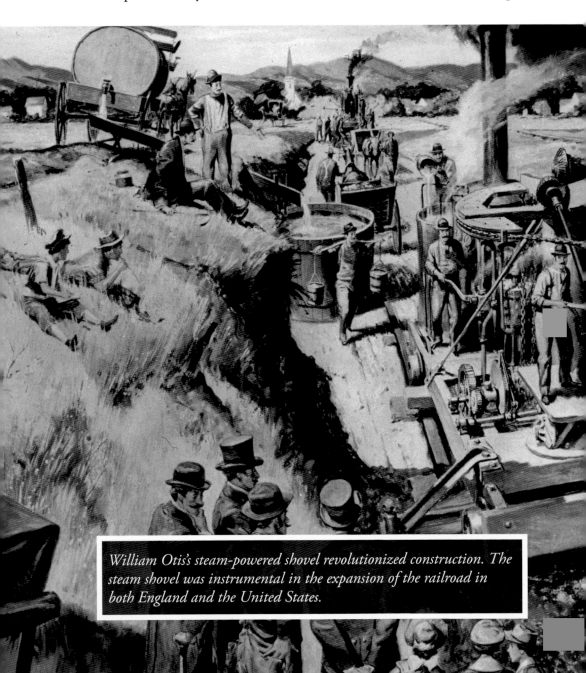

William Otis's steam-powered shovel revolutionized construction. The steam shovel was instrumental in the expansion of the railroad in both England and the United States.

powered by steam but by early versions of the diesel engines used on today's sites. It lives on in the excavator and all of the other heavy equipment it inspired.

OPERATIONAL ENGINEERING TODAY

Improvements in technology have changed the field of operational engineering. For example, today's hybrid engines release fewer greenhouse gasses, resulting in the preservation of workers' health.

The engine is not the only part of a vehicle that can be improved, however. Technology has made it easier to drive and maneuver heavy equipment.

Since the second half of the twentieth century, computers have become more common in engineering and construction. Instead of carrying rolls of blueprints, engineers can access them all on a tablet or laptop. Survey technicians use GPS (Global Positioning System) to figure out the elevation of survey areas. Equipment operators can use the same technology to make sure they smooth and grade in the right location as closely as possible. The use of GPS on job sites increases productivity.

Computers are also used to

PLAN AHEAD

Since becoming an operating or stationary engineer requires a great deal of training, it may be good to work ahead. High school offers a great chance to take some elective classes that could make getting an apprenticeship or job easier.

Math. Math is absolutely necessary in this profession! Operating and stationary engineers use math up to and including trigonometry (the study of triangles and their angles).

Physics. Physics is the study of how matter moves and reacts to outside forces. If boilers and heavy equipment are involved, it's good to understand physics.

Chemistry. Chemistry is the science of matter and how it forms and changes. Stationary engineers use chemistry in boiler work.

Computers. Computers are extremely important. Operating and stationary engineers must have a solid knowledge of computers. Programming skills are not necessary, but they could only help.

This knowledge is not a requirement for beginning an operating or stationary engineer career. It could, however, make you more competitive when applying for an apprenticeship.

control vehicles. Many of today's cranes come with wireless remote controls, which is a big change in the industry. This allows a crane operator to lift and move building materials more safely. Being outside the vehicle also makes it easier to see where loads are going.

STATIONARY ENGINEERING TODAY

Let's think of making electricity as simply as possible. All parts of a plant are important, but nothing could happen without the use of steam. Steam is the driving force of this entire process.

We need some sort of fuel to make steam. Think of a kettle that you use to boil water in your kitchen. When the water inside is heated, it becomes steam. The steam expands in the kettle and escapes through a vent somewhere near the spout. If there was no way for the steam to escape, the kettle could possibly explode. At the least, the steam and hot water could cause serious burns.

Now imagine a water tank that can hold the contents of thousands of kettles. We have just described a basic boiler. Instead of venting steam into the air, steam from a boiler is sent to a steam turbine. This is the device that replaced the steam engine in power plants. A turbine is made up of a long rod and a series of blades that rotate. When steam from the boiler reaches the steam turbine, the turbine begins to spin. The turbine is connected to a generator, which also spins to create electricity. From there, the electricity is sent to your home or your future stationary engineering office.

Once steam passes through the turbine, it is redirected, cooled off, and sent back to the boiler, where the process starts all over again. This is called a closed system.

The water inside a boiler is not your basic tap water. It is called feedwater, and it is treated with various chemicals to prevent rust and to create the best conditions for producing power with steam. Even though chemicals are added to feedwater, minerals in the water can still form scales that stick to the sides of the boiler. If the scales sink to the bottom they can create a thick paste called mud or sludge. To prevent this, boilers are "blown down," or cleaned out, regularly.

Generating electricity is the first part of this cycle. After electricity is created, is has to be sent out to homes and businesses. This is called distribution. Electricity leaves the generator and is converted to power that can be safely used by

FUELS OF THE FUTURE

The supply of fuels we use today to fire furnaces and run heavy equipment is limited. Coal, oil, and natural gas may not go away tomorrow, but we won't be able to use them forever. They also pollute our air, affect our climate, and cause breathing problems. We need other options that are safer. We need alternative and more sustainable fuels.

The Environmental Protection Agency (EPA) understands this and makes regulations to protect our environment. Regulations are specific rules on how to help keep our air and water clean. In Canada, the Alternative Fuels Act was passed in 1995 to get alternative fuels into common use more quickly in order to reduce greenhouse gases and pollution. It will take time for industries to make the switch, but these laws and regulations are a great start to cleaning up and maintaining our environment. The development of alternative fuels is also great news for workers who may spend up to twelve hours a day breathing in emissions from heavy equipment.

One alternative fuel in use today is an organic fuel called biodiesel. "Organic" means that it is made from plant and animal products. Biodiesel can be obtained from vegetable oil, animal fats, or even recycled oil from restaurants! McDonald's reported that it recycled 90 percent of its cooking oil worldwide in 2013. Not all of it went into the making of biodiesel, but even some of the largest companies on earth are participating.

Biodiesel can be blended with diesel fuel (up to 20 percent) and used in vehicles that only use diesel. Biodiesel can also completely power a vehicle, but the engine would have to be modified for it to work. On construction and job sites, most heavy equipment runs on gasoline or diesel fuel. Diesel fuel produces fewer contaminants than gasoline but still contributes to air pollution. Eventually making the switch to biodiesel would make for cleaner air at thousands of job sites.

Alternative fuels not used to generate electricity are important to stationary engineers, also. Diesel engines run much of the equipment in mechanical rooms: diesel-powered pumps, air compressors, and backup electrical generators can be found in mechanical rooms of schools, hospitals, malls, and other buildings.

transformers. From there it travels through the power lines and towers we see over our heads to factories and living rooms around North America. According to the U.S. Energy Information Administration, there are almost 20,000 generators operating at 7,300 power plants in the United States. Canada has more than 100.

THE FUTURE OF OPERATIONAL ENGINEERING

Some construction vehicles are now run by natural gas. Although it is a fossil fuel, natural gas burns more cleanly than coal and oil, and it costs less than either. There are some drawbacks, though. It costs a few thousand dollars to convert a standard engine to accept natural gas. New heavy-duty vehicles powered by natural gas engines are available, but some companies may choose to wait to upgrade until it's time to buy new equipment.

Drones will play a part in the future of operational engineering. Drones are small remote-controlled aircraft that are equipped with cameras. Using drones on work sites would make it much easier to inspect equipment in high places. This could mean less danger of workplace falls, which could save lives, time, and money. Drones could also be used to take pictures of large areas of land. This would be a great help to

An unmanned drone films men working on the jib of a tower crane high above a construction site. The use of drones by operational engineers will become more commonplace in the near future.

surveying technicians. As of 2015, drones are allowed on some sites in both Canada and the United States.

Prefabrication is another trend that will continue in the future. By fabricating, or making, larger items in advance, companies can bring them to sites in larger pieces. One piece could be a small house or restaurant—this could be a huge help for victims of hurricanes and other natural disasters.

One recent development that may change the way people work is 3D printing. This involves the printing of three-dimensional objects. The technology for 3D printing is still expensive but if it is integrated on job sites, the possibilities could be incredible. Broken parts could be replaced on the spot in an hour instead of days. The money saved on shipping and transport would be enormous.

An engineer at Boundary Dam power plant in Estevan, Saskatchewan, Canada, uses computers to monitor the capture and storage of carbon dioxide gas to keep it from entering the atmosphere.

Aside from the changes discussed, there are other trends that cannot be predicted. They may change the industry in ways no one can imagine. Some are being tested in labs, and some are still ideas on paper in an engineer's sketchbook. Whatever the idea or concept, be sure that operating engineers will be among the first in line to learn and apply that technology to their jobs.

THE FUTURE OF STATIONARY ENGINEERING

Beside alternative fuels, the fuel used to light and keep boilers fired will always concern stationary engineers. Knowing that the world's supply of fossil fuels is limited makes the future an exciting time in this field. We do not know where new fuels will come from, but the search for new forms of energy is a challenge that could improve the world.

The Boundary Dam project in Saskatchewan, Canada, opened in the fall of 2014. This is the world's first "clean coal" power plant. The coal itself is not clean, but the generation of electricity is. The plant is unique because it captures carbon dioxide (CO_2) and stores it to prevent it from entering the atmosphere. Carbon dioxide is found in nature, and it is also given off when fossil fuels are burned. Some of this CO_2 will be used in other industries such as oil drilling. A few plants are planned, but this technology is still expensive. As costs decrease, it may be used more and more. This means less and less damage to our environment. An EPA study shows that 37 percent of the world's carbon dioxide emissions come from electrical generation. Reducing those emissions would be a huge step for the energy industry.

The future of stationary engineering also includes looking backward. One technology from the past that has uses for the future is cogeneration. Cogeneration was first used in 1882 at Thomas Edison's Pearl Street Station, the first central control station in the world. The six steam engines that supplied power also warmed the homes of its customers for every year that it remained open.

Like its name suggests, cogeneration is very closely linked to electrical generation. By adding extra steps, cogeneration plants can make power generation even more efficient. They burn less fuel by basically recycling the exhaust from making electricity. The heat from turbines and engines can be saved and used to heat water, make steam, and provide heat to homes. Many power plants can be changed to become cogeneration plants. The cost varies from plant to plant, but it could cost millions of dollars to do. That may not sound cheap, but the good that cogeneration can do the environment may be worth the money.

Some of the most energy-efficient ways to generate electricity, like ocean thermal energy conversion (OTEC), are still too expensive. If the cost can be brought down on this and other types of technology, generating power in the future may look completely different than it does today.

chapter 3

HEAVY EQUIPMENT

We have learned that operating engineers use heavy equipment. But what is heavy equipment, exactly? According to the International Union of Operating Engineers (IUOE), if a vehicle "rolls on tires or crawls on tracks like a tank," or if a machine can "push, pull, pump, or lift material," then it is heavy equipment. This is a broad definition, but it works because there are dozens of vehicles and machines that can be used by operating engineers.

Some operating engineers are called hoisting and portable engineers because they spend the majority of their time working with machines that hoist (lift) and move large heavy objects. A crane operator is a good example of a hoisting engineer.

Heavy equipment operators and mechanics are often found on construction sites. They operate large vehicles and machines that are necessary to complete a variety of jobs, including building (erecting schools and skyscrapers, for example) and repairing (bridges and roadways).

Some other machines that operating engineers use on site include cranes, bulldozers, front-end loaders, rollers, backhoes, graders, dredges, hoists, pumps, and compressors. Operating engineers may need to be able to operate more than one of these machines since many different pieces of equipment may be needed for a single project.

JOB DESCRIPTION

If you decide to work with heavy equipment, prepare to get messy. This is a world of dirt, grease, and grime. This job can be a physical workout, too. Some vehicles require climbing ladders or steps to enter and may be hundreds of feet above the ground.

Your brain will be challenged, also. Engineers who work with heavy equipment need to read and understand diagrams, manuals, and blueprints.

A construction road crew excavates earth for a highway project during a night work shift. Operating engineers often have to work at night on intimidating equipment.

kdays usually last from ten to twelve hours. Projects
nd end, so expect to travel to different work sites.
a car or some type of reliable transportation is extremely
Some jobs may last only a day or two while larger proj-
last for years.

ge quantity of work is performed during the day, but
ork is also common for people working with heavy
ery on bridges, highways, and other traffic-related job
eather can be a factor in this field, especially heavy rain,
id ice, but this depends on location.

Construction equipment operators are often
found moving something. Some experience driving
or operating street or farm vehicles could be helpful. Control is incredibly important when operating
heavy equipment. These are skills that can be
learned and perfected as an apprentice, however.

Much of the machinery used in construction is
heavy and dangerous. Heavy equipment operators
need to be able to use construction vehicles to perform various tasks, including digging, lifting,
loading, drilling, hoisting, and pumping.

Construction equipment operators must be
good at driving and controlling machines, but their
skills only matter if they have vehicles to drive. To
keep heavy equipment in safe working condition,
most have some training in the maintenance of the
equipment they are certified to operate. But when
machinery breaks down, other operating engineers
are needed to perform necessary repairs. Heavy
vehicle technicians are the mechanics who diagnose
and fix mechanical problems. Much of this work
involves using computers or computerized equipment to locate and repair heavy equipment
problems. A strong knowledge of tools is also

necessary. Many heavy vehicle technicians purchase their own hand tools over the course of their careers, which can cost thousands of dollars. Heavy vehicles have many different systems. Technicians should be familiar with and able to repair electrical and hydraulic systems in vehicles as well as their engines.

A heavy equipment repairperson makes adjustments to the engine of an excavator. Heavy vehicle technicians must be able to diagnose and solve problems with machinery.

EDUCATION AND TRAINING

A high school diploma or GED is required to become a construction equipment operator or heavy vehicle service technician. Classes in electronics, shop (industrial arts), and auto repair would be helpful. In addition to formal classes, thousands of hours of experience are needed to operate and repair heavy equipment. These are not skills you can teach yourself.

Those wanting to be vehicle operators and mechanics can obtain training in a few ways. Some private construction and mining companies offer on-the-job training that can provide valuable experience driving or repairing vehicles. Combined with classroom training, this experience can lead to employment.

Private trade and vocational schools sometimes offer tuition assistance. They can also offer help in finding employment after a program is completed. Before you pay a school money for tuition, make sure you have explored all the options. Some veterans of the armed forces may qualify for either the post-9/11 GI Bill or the Montgomery GI Bill. Both give eligible former military personnel help with educational costs.

Make sure to conduct some preliminary research before you sign up for a class or course of study. Classroom work is only part of this process. It is usually necessary to find some sort of instruction that combines traditional teaching with training on the job. Also check with a school or institution to make sure that its certificates or qualifications are accepted by businesses and companies in your area. Trade unions are another way to obtain entry-level work. The IUOE says, "the [apprentice] system is designed to give someone who knows little or nothing about the trade the knowledge to become a journey-level operating engineer."

Apprentices begin work at a local union, or chapter, that trains and represents all of the union employees in a geographical area. They work under more experienced operating engineers who are known as journeypersons. Apprentices usually start out earning around half of a journeyperson's salary. As they continue to train,

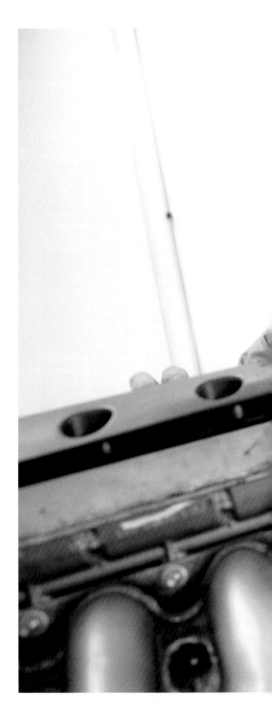

Future mechanics work on an automobile engine under the watchful eye of their instructor. Most programs offer classroom experience combined with practical apprenticeships.

THE JOB CORPS

Another way to become an operating or stationary engineer is through Job Corps. This division of the U.S. Department of Labor wants to "help young people ages 16 through 24 improve the quality and satisfaction of their lives through vocational and academic training." This means that the Job Corps can provide young people with the skills and training they need to enter a technical career.

This program is specifically for low-income students and provides assistance for every aspect of the job-hunting process. The Job Corps provides classes for students to earn a GED or high school diploma, training for technical careers, and job placement after training.

After graduation, Job Corps participants can also get help with college admissions, job searches, housing, and child care.

Students who are accepted serve anywhere from eight months to two years. One hundred percent of room and board and tuition are paid for, in addition to a small allowance. One thing to be aware of: not all centers offer the same classes, so you may have to travel elsewhere to pursue a specialty.

apprentices' salaries will rise. Apprentices normally stay on after completing their training. According to the IUOE, by the end of training apprentices can earn up to 90 percent of a journeyperson's salary. As they work, union employees pay dues, which go into a fund that helps pay for health care and retirement.

Update training is regularly given to union members free of charge. For a fee, nonunion members can take the same courses. Training equipment will vary from local to local. Some have large indoor simulators for heavy equipment training.

CERTIFICATIONS AND LICENSES

Many states and provinces require a commercial driver's license (CDL). This kind of license enables a person to drive both multiple trailer trucks and trucks that transport hazardous materials. In the United States, a CDL has reciprocity with Canada. This means that Canadian and U.S. license holders need only one license to drive in both countries.

Since certification requirements vary from state to state, it is best to check with your state or province to see if it requires specialized licenses for particular pieces of equipment. Some larger cities may also ask for additional or special qualifications.

JOB OUTLOOK

In the coming years, heavy equipment operators in construction can look forward to more job opportunities than in other professions. An increasing population in the United States and Canada means a natural increase in the need for housing, schools, and similar buildings. Over

An operator-in-training learns how to operate a track loader on the job. With an increasing need to build and repair infrastructure, opportunities will be plentiful.

the next twenty years, thousands of repairs must be made to North America's infrastructure (dams, highways, and bridges, for example). The median pay for this profession is $40,980 per year ($19.70 per hour). "Median" means that half of the people in this field will earn less than this number and the other half will earn more.

The job outlook for heavy vehicle service technicians is positive also. Jobs are expected to grow almost 9 percent, according to the Bureau of Labor Statistics. This is about average when compared to all other jobs examined by the U.S. Department of Labor. The median pay for heavy equipment mechanics is $43,820 per year ($21.07 per hour).

Both specialties depend on a strong economy to succeed. Slow or down times in the economy can put a halt to construction and repair projects that have been either planned or started. Pay for both also depends on location. Workers in urban areas tend to earn slightly higher rates than tradespersons in areas with fewer people, likely due to a higher cost of living.

chapter 4

SURVEYING

Surveying technicians, or map technicians, are operating engineers that assist land surveyors and mapmakers. They measure angles, distances and elevation, and other data. These measurements are then used to set boundaries for construction and to make maps. Surveying technicians may also work with photogrammetrists (people who make measurements from photographs to create maps).

A survey technician measures elevation with a theodolite. Surveying is one specialty of operating engineering. Surveying technicians measure and record data for construction and maps.

Survey technicians work with computers on a daily basis and must be comfortable with advanced engineering and design software and database software.

Like most operating engineers, some survey technicians can expect to spend a large part of their workday outside. This work may be on bridges, highways, or any number of construction or work sites. Some technicians may work indoors if they are processing surveying measurements using computers.

This kind of work is very precise and requires complex equipment. Most of these tools are heavy, fragile, and expensive. The theodolite, which is used to take precise measurement on a site, can cost up to $5,000! Tools like this also take training to operate and maintain. New technology and equipment will require additional training.

Math is essential to this profession. Survey technicians need an excellent knowledge of different areas of mathematics, including algebra, geometry, trigonometry, calculus, and statistics. Much of the work in this job requires quick and accurate calculations. A steady hand is also required—some of measurements in this profession are recorded to fractions of inches.

Organizational skills are also expected; surveying requires taking extensive and accurate notes. Survey technicians should be able to read maps and diagrams and be familiar with geography, the science of the earth's features and landscape.

Communication is a very important aspect of the profession. At times, calculations and measurements may need to be translated and explained to other people on a project.

EDUCATION AND TRAINING

Survey technicians, like heavy equipment operators and mechanics, must have a high school diploma or GED to enter the profession. The pathways to employment in this line of work are similar to those for other operating engineers. Union

The measurements taken by survey technicians inform architectural drawings. These plans contain all of the details and instructions necessary for a construction crew to complete a project to specification.

apprenticeships can pay a partial salary, but it is always good to investigate this with individual employers who are affiliated with unions.

Two operating engineers determine the initial survey boundaries of a site. Most of the work of survey technicians is done outdoors, which is a bonus for those who don't like to sit behind a desk all day.

CERTIFICATIONS AND LICENSES

Many states and provinces require a certified survey technician (CST) license to work as a technician. Some third-party associations and societies offer licenses as well. Before you apply for any license or certification, make sure you can use it where you plan to live and work. Sometimes, being in possession of a CST license can earn you a higher fee.

JOB OUTLOOK

The future job outlook for survey technicians is good. The Bureau of Labor Statistics predicts the job will grow by 15 percent over the next ten years. The median salary as of 2012 is $39,670 per year ($19.07 per hour).

chapter 5

BOILERS AND HVACR

W hile operating engineers spend their time in the great outdoors, stationary engineers can usually be found behind the scenes keeping the world running. Basement equipment rooms are more likely workspaces for them. Boiler operators and HVACR (heating, ventilation, air-conditioning, and refrigeration) mechanics are stationary engineers that need to bring math skills, attention to detail, and physical stamina to their spaces each and every day.

Without the work of stationary engineers, we would miss many of the benefits of modern life we take for granted. Boiler operators perform the first steps of electrical generation. Without the electrical power they help create and maintain, the world would be a less comfortable and darker place.

HVACR mechanics are also responsible for our comfort and survival; they keep our air breathable, hot equipment cool, and cold people warm.

A stationary engineer measures gauge readings in a boiler room and records them. Stationary engineers often work deep in the basements of large buildings.

JOB DESCRIPTION

Many stationary engineers' jobs are essential; they must be done around the clock. Power plants do not shut down at the end of a workday—they operate every hour of every day. Much of the equipment in mechanical rooms cannot be turned on in a matter of minutes. Dozens of checks must be made on boilers and engines before they can be powered up. Mechanical rooms or electrical spaces with running equipment must always be monitored and maintained.

Bad weather does not affect indoor machinery; workers in such spaces are expected to be at work and on time, no matter the weather. Many stationary engineers find employment in hospitals, factories, or office buildings.

The work life of many HVACR and boiler engineers involves shift work. Since many pieces of equipment are on for long periods of time, a nine-to-five workday is uncommon. An average shift is approximately eight hours. Some shifts are overnight, and some take place during the day. Having a shift in the middle of the night doesn't mean that that will be your shift forever, though. Shifts are rotated, or changed, over time. Despite the different hours, you can expect a forty-hour work week. Both boiler operators and HVACR mechanics can expect to crawl around and get dirty because most machinery associated with boilers and HVACR equipment is located in hard-to-reach places.

Boiler operators are the engineers who ensure boilers are in working condition. This can cover all of the processes associated with boilers, as well as repair and maintenance of other machinery in a space.

HVACR mechanics and installers work with heating, cooling, and refrigeration systems. Some of this work is outside; many AC and heating units can be found on the roofs of hotels and sports arenas. This may be the most computer-intensive

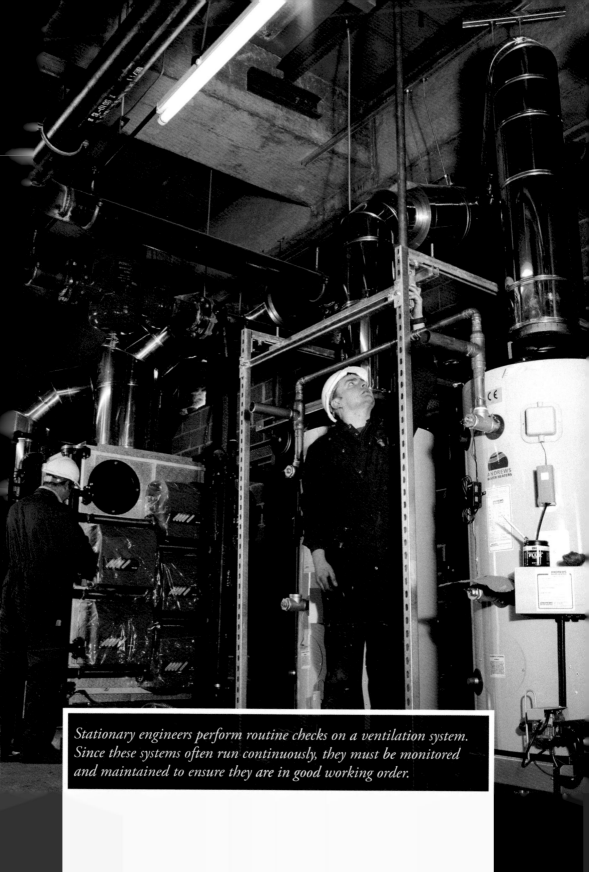

Stationary engineers perform routine checks on a ventilation system. Since these systems often run continuously, they must be monitored and maintained to ensure they are in good working order.

job for a stationary engineer. Many HVACR systems are completely computerized and made up of hundreds of sensors. Each sensor is a tiny computer that can monitor temperature, air quality, and ventilation in a particular room or area. Together, they can be controlled by a building automation system, or BAS. Building automation makes it possible to monitor lighting, heat, and other mechanical and electrical equipment in a large building from one central location. For example, BAS makes it possible to change the temperature and turn off lights in individual rooms remotely, rather than one at a time. Buildings that rely on BAS are often called "smart buildings."

Both boiler operators and HVACR mechanics need to be familiar with the basic principals of mechanical and electrical systems. This includes maintenance and repair. Any experience with small tools, chemistry, and math would very good skills to have before training for these careers.

An HVACR technician performs maintenance on a rooftop air-conditioning system. While HVACR systems can be computerized, the job still requires mechanical aptitude.

BEYOND FOSSIL FUELS

Although we've focused on using fossil fuels like coal, oil, and natural gas to heat boilers and create electricity, there are many other fuel sources on, below, and above the earth. Many of these sources are renewable or sustainable:

Nuclear energy is in use in power plants today. Nuclear energy is released when one atom is split into two. The large amount of heat that results fires the boiler to make steam. This is called nuclear fusion. The heat from nuclear energy is cleaner that fossil fuels but it leaves behind radioactive waste that is difficult to store safely. Some states and parts of Canada classify nuclear energy as renewable.

Solar energy uses the sun's energy to heat a liquid that is then used to heat a boiler to make electricity.

Wind energy uses the power of the wind to move a group of wind turbines. The turbines can then move a generator for power.

Geothermal energy uses the heat below us to generate power. There are pockets of hot water under the earth's surface. This water is much hotter (the lowest temperature is about 400°F, or 204.4°C) than our lakes and rivers; it is constantly heated by the earth and released as steam. The steam powers a turbine and electricity is made.

Ocean thermal energy conversion (OTEC). Water at lower depths in the ocean is much colder that water near the surface. This temperature difference is used to heat liquids to drive turbines to generate electricity. Energy from the ocean doesn't produce any harmful gases, but it is more expensive than other fuel sources.

EDUCATION AND TRAINING

The best way to obtain training as a stationary engineer today is through an apprenticeship with a union. An apprenticeship can be a kind of "one-stop shop" for young people who would like to pursue these careers. Apprentices receive on-the-job training and about 50 percent of the pay they could expect to earn as a journeyperson.

Some cities and large town's look to unions for personnel to work as stationary engineers in public facilities. Private schools and community colleges are still valid ways to get an education, but finding employment afterward may be more challenging. Also, on-the-job training may be harder to locate for some stationary engineers. Another possibility is enlisting in the navy or Merchant Marine. Both supply room and board to trainees throughout their studies. Boilers and HVACR equipment are very similar at sea and on land.

A stationary engineer apprenticeship lasts four years with about six hundred hours of classroom training. Apprentices work under journeyperson-level boiler tenders or stationary engineers. Training is not limited to boilers; the course work includes HVACR, chemistry, physics, electricity and electronics, and welding.

Upon completing an apprenticeship, the next level of proficiency is journeyperson. After a few years in that position, opportunities to train apprentices may arise. Throughout this time, update training on equipment is usually given.

Assistant engineers have even more experience. They assist chief engineers with managing engineering and machinery rooms as they continue to train. Over time, this increased training

Two HVACR technicians perform repairs to an inoperative cooling unit. Working on HVACR systems often involves standing on a rooftop in all kinds of weather conditions.

and knowledge will give assistant engineers the necessary skills to take on even more responsibility and salary in this profession.

CERTIFICATIONS AND LICENSES

Certification titles can vary by location. Some states may have four levels of certification for stationary engineers, and some may have three. Looking at what knowledge is needed for each is the best way to determine which certification you may need. Check with your state's Department of Labor to find this information.

Canada has five levels of certification. The lower the number, the lower the experience and responsibility. Typically, workers with a third-class certification have the experience level of a journeyperson.

JOB OUTLOOK

Job growth for boiler operators is expected to be slow. The BLS expects 3 percent growth, which is lower than the number of projected opportunities for operating engineers. The median salary is expected to be $53,560 per year ($25.75 per hour).

Prospects are excellent for HVACR technicians. Even if there is a slowdown in the construction or power industries, existing buildings and equipment still need heating, cooling, and clean air. Additionally, HVACR equipment is becoming more complex and relies more on computers than previously. The BLS says a growth of 21 percent can be expected in coming years.

The median salary for HVACR mechanics and installers is $43,640 per year ($20.98 per hour).

chapter 6

BUILDING MANAGEMENT

After spending a significant amount of time in their jobs, stationary engineers gather enough knowledge about all types of equipment found in large mechanical rooms and power plants. At this point, they have enough experience to manage all of the machinery in a space on a shift.

Valves and fittings in boiler rooms and mechanical spaces must be frequently checked for proper operation. This kind of maintenance is ultimately the building manager's responsibility.

Management at this level involves much more than repair skills and equipment knowledge. Some jobs require new skills. For example, a building manager at a hotel may have to learn customer service in order to deal with customers directly. A chief engineer at a prison may need to make sure steam is available for laundry and industrial use.

A first-class stationary engineer's license and at least ten to twelve years of experience are needed to reach this level of employment. Jobs at this stage have titles such as building engineer, maintenance foreman, and chief engineer, and responsibilities are often determined by work experience.

At this point, stationary engineers can begin to really specialize. Facility types vary from industry to industry. Some are new and changing rapidly, and some are more standardized. Job listings are a great source of information on first-class engineer responsibilities for specific job environments.

SEVEN QUESTIONS WITH RUSSELL DUKE

Russell Duke is the director of Stationary Affairs at the IUOE. He has worked in this position since 2005.

1. What do you do at your job?
I make sure all the local chapters of our union have the most up-to-date and accurate training resources.

2. Does the union write training guides and material?
We do a lot of it on our own, but we also get input from local union subject matter experts.

3. Is stationary engineering challenging?

Yes, it is! Challenging but rewarding. You never have the same day twice. Something is always going on, and that's exciting to engineers. We enjoy troubleshooting and solving problems.

4. Do computers play a large part in your work?

We've been using computers constantly since the 1980s. They help monitor and control equipment.

5. Could computers eventually replace stationary engineers?

It was a concern in the early days of computer control for buildings. Stationary engineers adapt to new technologies. We have found that computers enhance our work, but even if a computer could do many of our tasks, we would still need engineers to maintain and repair the mechanical equipment as well as the computers themselves.

6. What kind of classes should students take in high school that might prepare them for a career in stationary engineering?

Math is very important—stationary engineers use lots of basic math, some algebra, and some trigonometry. Physics is great to learn too. If your school offers these, I recommend taking any of the following: HVAC[R], plumbing (including soldering and brazing), arc welding, shop classes, mechanical drawing, basic electricity, and earth science.

7. What advice would you give someone who wanted to have a career as a stationary engineer?

If you don't mind getting your hands dirty and you like to work hard, you can really succeed in this profession!

This may be a supervisory role, but training is still a large part of the job. Building and chief engineers may be responsible for the training of their staff. They are often required to monitor qualifications and hold training with team members as technology or job requirements change.

JOB OUTLOOK

The average salary for building managers and chief engineers is $75,437, according to www.payscale.com. Pay depends on many factors at this stage of achievement. These factors include the amount of equipment being overseen, the quantity of employees managed, and the number and extent of spaces to oversee. Another factor may be the type of of business housed in the building run by the building manager or chief engineer.

Chief engineers must oversee the operations of a building or a building's systems. This position requires many years in the field and extensive knowledge of the systems.

A CHANGING PROFESSION

Operating and stationary engineers have complex jobs that require proficiency in math, science, and computer technology. Every day can be a completely new experience involving problem solving and quick thinking. Entering either profession takes dedication and attention to hundreds of tiny details. Patience is also needed; the training for these jobs takes three to four years as an apprentice or trainee.

A high school diploma or GED is sufficient to begin the training process for most of these occupations. Learning does not stop for operating and stationary engineers. As some pieces of equipment age, new equipment and techniques replace them. Update training occurs throughout a career. This is essential because it increases both safety and job performance.

Chief engineers and building managers are responsible for the running of all of the machinery and equipment in a building, as well as the management of the building's engineers and technicians.

All of the professions discussed in this resource require some discipline. The hours can be long and physically demanding. Most instructions must be followed exactly and be done in a specific time. Dependability is a must; no matter how skilled an engineer may be, he or she must be on time and ready to work. Overall, prospects for the future are positive for these jobs. Skilled labor is in demand and will be for the next ten years. More women and minorities are entering these fields through scholarships, grants, and organizations such as Job Corps and trade unions.

As the needs of society change, so do the jobs of operating and stationary engineers. New machines, energy sources, and construction methods have the potential to change the way jobs are done. In this line of work, adapting to challenges as they happen is normal. The dedicated men and women who have chosen these professions do not have glamorous jobs, but they provide crucial services that help us work, play, and live.

glossary

apprentice A person who receives both classroom and on-the-job training to learn a trade.

apprenticeship The time an apprentice spends studying and training for a trade under the guidance of a journeyperson.

automation Using computers to monitor and adjust different parts of a system from one location.

boiler A large metal container used to heat water until it becomes steam. The steam is then used to move a generator to create electricity.

electrical energy Using generated electricity to create heat, light, and motion.

engineering The profession of using science and math to design, build, and operate vehicles, bridges, roads, machines, and more.

feedwater Water that is treated with chemicals and pumped into a boiler to create steam.

fossil fuel A fuel that has been created by nature over millions of years. Examples would be coal, natural gas, and oil.

furnace The chamber used to heat the liquid in a boiler.

generator A large magnet wrapped in copper wire that creates electricity when it spins at high speeds.

grade How much an area of land slants or slopes. This is usually measured by a surveyor.

HVACR Heating, ventilation (or ventilating), air-conditioning, and refrigeration.

infrastructure Basic services and facilities necessary for a society to work, including bridges, tunnels, and water and sewer services.

journeyperson A person who works with and gives apprentices on-the-job training as they learn a trade.

matter Anything that takes up space and has mass (weight).

mechanical room A room or rooms on a ship or in a large building where boilers, chillers, HVAC, and other machinery are kept.

Merchant Marine A fleet of civilian ships that help carry troops and supplies for their country's military during wartime.

renewable resources Sources of energy that are replaced by nature such as wind, sunlight, and waves.

survey To inspect and map a portion of the earth's surface.

system A collection of machines or processes that all contribute to a larger result, i.e. a power plant.

trade A job that involves a specialized skill that must be taught in the classroom and through practice.

trade union A group of skilled workers from the same industry that ensures training, fair pay, health care, and safe working conditions for its members.

turbine A machine that connects a boiler and a generator. Steam spins the turbine, which in turn spins a generator to create electricity.

vocational school A school that trains students for technical careers.

for more information

International Union of Operating Engineers (IUOE)
1125 17th Street NW
Washington, DC 20036
(202) 741-7747
Website: http://www.iuoe.org
IUOE is a trade union that serves members in the both the
    United States and Canada.

Job Corps Recruiting
200 Constitution Avenue NW, Suite N4463
Washington, DC 20210
(202) 693-3000
Website: https://recruiting.jobcorps.gov
Job Corps is a technical job-training program that helps more
    than sixty thousand students per year.

National Association of Stationary Operating Engineers
    (NASOE)
212 Elmwood Avenue Ext., Suite 500
Gloversville, NY 12078
(518) 620-3683
Website: http://nasoe.org
NASOE is a national third-party organization that provides
    testing and licensing for stationary engineers.

Royal Canadian Navy
Leonce Lessard Building
1420 Saint-Catherine Street W.
Montreal, QB H3G 1R3
Canada

(800) 856-8488
Website: http://forces.ca
The Royal Canadian Navy offers marine engineering training
    that can help with jobs outside of the military.

Seafarers International Union, Atlantic, Gulf, Lakes & Inland
    Waters
5201 Auth Way
Camp Springs, MD 20746
(301) 899-0675
Website: http://www.seafarers.org
Sefarers offers an entry program and job assistance for
    students who may want to explore membership in the
    Merchant Marine.

United States Navy
Navy Recruiting Command
5722 Integrity Drive
Building 784
Millington, TN 38054
(800) USA-NAVY (872-6289)
Website: http://navy.com
The navy offers programs in marine and applied sciences for
    enlisted personnel; the skills can make finding a skilled job
    easier afterward.

WEBSITES

Because of the changing nature of Internet links, Rosen
Publishing has developed an online list of websites related to
the subject of this book. This site is updated regularly. Please
use this link to access the list:
http://www.rosenlinks.com/ECAR/Oper

for further reading

Baine, Celeste. *Is There an Engineer Inside You? A Comprehensive Guide to Career Decisions in Engineering* (4th edition). Springfield, OR: Engineering Education Service Center, 2013.

Bickerstaff, Linda. *Careers in Heating, Ventilation, and Air-Conditioning (HVAC)*. New York, NY: Rosen Publishing, 2014.

Ching, Francis D. K. *Building Construction Illustrated*. Hoboken, NJ: Wiley, 2014.

Ferguson editors. *Careers in Focus: Energy*. New York, NY: Ferguson's, an imprint of Infobase Learning, 2012.

Gibilisco, Stan. *Electricity Demystified*. New York, NY: McGraw-Hill Professional, 2012.

Godsell, Ryan. *Electricity Power Systems: A Comprehensive Guide for Students and Professionals* (Electrical Engineering Book 3). Seattle, WA. Ryco Kindle Publishing, 2014.

Haddock, Keith. *Modern Earthmoving Machines: Bulldozers, Wheel Loaders, Bucket Wheels, Scrapers, Graders, Excavators, Off-Road Haulers, and Walking Draglines*. Los Altos, CA: Enthusiast Books, 2011.

Huzij, Robert. *Modern Diesel Technology: Heavy Equipment Systems*. Boston, MA: Cengage Learning, 2013.

Jackson, Barbara J. *Construction Management JumpStart: The Best First Step Toward a Career in Construction Management*. San Francisco, CA: Sybex, 2010.

Jones and Bartlett Learning. *Ugly's Electrical References*. Burlington, MA: Jones and Bartlett Learning, 2014.

Kavanagh, Barry, and Diane K. Slattery. *Surveying with Construction Applications* (8th edition). Upper Saddle River, NJ: Prentice Hall, 2014.

Lewis, Anna M. *Women of Steel and Stone: 22 Inspirational Architects, Engineers, and Landscape Designers.* Chicago, IL: Chicago Review Press, 2014.

Masters, Nancy Robinson. *Heavy Equipment Operator.* Ann Arbor, MI: Cherry Lake Pub., 2011.

Morkes, Andrew G., ed. *Nontraditional Careers for Women and Men: More Than 25 Great Jobs for Women and Men with Apprenticeships Through PhDs.* Markham, Ontario: International Press Publications, Inc., 2011.

Passbooks. *Heavy Equipment Operator.* Syosset, NY: National Learning Corporation, 2014.

Wohlfarth, Ray. *Lessons Learned in a Boiler Room: A Common Sense Approach to Servicing and Installing Commercial Boilers.* White Bear Lake, MN: Fire and Ice, 2011.

Yomtov, Nelson. *Water/Wastewater Engineer.* Ann Arbor, MI: Cherry Lane Publishing, 2015.

bibliography

"Construction Equipment Operators." Bureau of Labor Statistics. Retrieved April 2, 2015 (http://www.bls.gov/ooh/construction-and-extraction/construction-equipment-operators.htm).

Engineering Mania 2. "Boiler Basics." YouTube. Retrieved April 5, 2015 (https://www.youtube.com/watch?v=WalH2o6JKu0).

Engineering Mania 2. "Basic Principles of Pressure and Temperature." YouTube. Retrieved April 5, 2015 (https://www.youtube.com/watch?v=T-q4gtWccW4).

Frost, Harold J, Daryl R. Frederick, and M. Steingress. *Stationary Engineering* (2008 Edition). Orland Park, IL: American Technical Publishers, Inc., 2008.

Goloboy, Jennifer Lee, ed. *Industrial Revolution: People and Perspectives* (Perspectives in American Social History). Santa Barbara, CA: ABC-CLIO, 2008.

"Heating, Air Conditioning, and Refrigeration Mechanics and Installers." Bureau of Labor Statistics. Retrieved April 2, 2015 (http://www.bls.gov/ooh/installation-mainte-nance-and-repair/heating-air-conditioning-and-refrigeration-mechanics-and-installers.htm).

"Heating, Air Conditioning, and Refrigeration Mechanics and Installers." O*Net OnLine. Retrieved April 2, 2015 (http://www.onetonline.org/link/summary/49-9021.00).

"Heavy Vehicle and Mobile Equipment Service Technicians." Bureau of Labor Statistics. Retrieved April 2, 2015 (http://www.bls.gov/ooh/installation-maintenance-and-repair/heavy-vehicle-and-mobile-equipment-service-technicians.html).

Hobsbawm, Eric, and Chris Wrigley, ed. *Industry and Empire: The Birth of the Industrial Revolution*. New York, NY: The New Press, 1999.

International Union of Operating Engineers. "The Field of Stationary Engineering." Retrieved April 28, 2015. PDF File.

Khalil, Essam E. *Air Distribution in Buildings* (Mechanical and Aerospace Engineering). Boca Raton, FL: CRC Press, 2013.

Miller, Rex, and Mark Miller. *HVAC Licensing Study Guide*, Second edition. New York, NY: McGraw-Hill Professional Publishing, 2012.

Sharma, Rakesh. "The Future of 3D Printing and Manufacturing." Forbes.com, January 15, 2014 (http://www.forbes.com/sites/rakeshsharma/2014/01/15/1255).

Smith Russell E. *Electricity for Refrigeration, Heating and Air Conditioning*. Clifton Park, NY: Delmar Cengage Learning, 2014.

Smith, Wayne B. *Boiler Operation* (Steam Plant Operations Book 1). Trinity, FL: LSA, 2012.

"Stationary Engineers and Boiler Operators." Bureau of Labor Statistics. Retrieved April 2, 2015 (http://www.bls.gov/ooh/production/stationary-engineers-and-boiler-operators.htm).

"Stationary Engineers and Boiler Operators." O*Net OnLine. Retrieved April 2, 2015 (http://www.onetonline.org/link/summary/51-8021.00).

Steingress, Frederick M., Harold J. Frost, and Daryl R. Walker. *High Pressure Boilers*. Orland Park, IL: American Technical Publishers, Inc., 2012.

Steingress, Frederick M., and Daryl R. Walker. *Low Pressure Boilers*. Orland Park, IL: American Technical Publishers, Inc., 2012.

Sugarman, Samuel C. *HVAC Fundamentals.* Lilburn, GA: The Fairmont Press, 2004.

"Surveying and Mapping Technicians." Bureau of Labor Statistics. Retrieved April 2, 2015 (http://www.bls.gov/ooh/architecture-and-engineering/surveying-and-mapping-technicians.htm).

index

ABOUT THE AUTHOR

Kerry Hinton has written several books for young adults. He studied naval engineering at the United States Naval Academy and spent the next five years in the U.S. Navy working as a damage control assistant. He learned most of what he knows from machinists, boiler technicians, mechanics, equipment operators, and all other sorts of marine engineers. He lives in Hoboken, New Jersey, with his wife.

PHOTO CREDITS

Cover, p. 1 (figures) foto infot/Shutterstock.com; cover, p. 1 (background) Christian Lagerek/Shutterstock.com; pp. 4-5, 61 © iStockphoto.com/nimis69; pp. 10-11, 34-35 © AP Images; p. 12 © Jim Zuckerman/Alamy; pp. 14-15 Alistair Berg/The Image Bank/Getty Images; pp. 16-17 Dmitry Kalinovsky/Shutterstock.com; p. 21 Library of Congress Prints and Photographs Division; p. 24 Kuznetcov_Konstantin/Shutterstock.com; pp. 26-27 Three Lions/Hulton Archive/Getty Images; pp. 32-33 © Ruskin Photos/Alamy; pp. 38-39 Ethan Welty/Aurora/ Getty Images; pp. 40-41, 64 Bloomberg/Getty Images; pp. 42-43 Goodluz/Shutterstock.com; p. 45 © Clarke Conde/ Alamy; p. 47 © iStockphoto.com/shotbydave; p. 49 Rehan Qureshi/Shutterstock.com; pp. 50-51 michaeljung/ Shutterstock.com; pp. 52-53 © iStockphoto.com/kaspiic; p. 55 © Peter Noyce CST/Alamy; p. 56 © iStockphoto. com/sturti; pp. 58-59 © ZUMA Press, Inc/Alamy; p. 65 © iStockphoto.com/kickstand

Designer: Matt Cauli; Editor: Christine Poolos; Photo Researcher: Nicole DiMella